Student's Guide to Corporate America

Student's Guide to Corporate America

By Greg Coleman

Table of Contents

1. Perception is Reality
2. Rules of Engagement
3. Visibility
4. Goals and Expectations
5. Protect Yourself at All Times
6. Communication
7. Surviving the Game
8. The Dangers of Yes
9. Culture is the Key
10. Impact of Initiative
11. Mentors

Students Guide to Corporate America

Introduction

Congratulations! If you are reading this you have graduated with your diploma, certification, or degree and are preparing to enter to white collar world known as Corporate America. Your dedication to your years of schooling has allowed you to trade in the hard hat and shovel of blue collar manual labor for the desk-driving, meeting-laden environment of Corporate America. After years of toiling in classrooms, pulling all-night study/cram sessions to prepare for multiple finals, and spending countless hours at the computer lab or library working on group projects you're finally free and it's time to actually get paid for all the work you do! Sounds pretty good right? Well as the old saying goes "Be careful what you wish for because you just might get it." The world you are about to enter is nothing like you have ever experienced before. The days where you and only you controlled your success, gone! The days of hard work paying off in good grades, no more! Most importantly, the days of knowing what's expected of you and how to be successful, fahgetaboutit!

The world you are about to enter no classroom, lab, or tutoring session has prepared you for. In this world, everything you have ever learned about success and what it looks like is flipped on its ear. In this world, politics and the ability to engage in them can make the difference between climbing the ladder and being stuck in professional purgatory. This can be extremely frustrating, confusing and downright discouraging for students entering this brave new world. This is what led me to write this book. I have experienced more than my fair share of ups and downs in Corporate America. One day I thought how nice would it have been if someone had educated me on what to expect and gave me advice on how to handle it. Therefore I am sharing my experiences in Corporate America with you and giving you tips and tricks on how to navigate the Corporate Jungle. Hopefully this will help you enjoy early success as you begin your career in a corporate setting and enjoy continued success as your progress up the corporate ladder. So without any further a due, let's get into it!

1. Perception is Reality!

I'm sure you have heard the saying that to some people perception is greater than reality. Well this saying goes a little bit differently in Corporate America. In the Corporate Jungle, Perception IS REALITY!! Now this might sound crazy that in an environment with some of the best and brightest professionals in the world but it's true. One would think, as I once mistakenly did, that in this environment where attention to detail is important that a manager/leader would do their due diligence before forming opinion about you or your work but guess what? THEY DON'T. If you take nothing else from this book, come to grips with and understand this very simple principle that will help you tremendously in your maiden voyage into Corporate America: It's not what you do, it's what they think you do. During my administrative residency for my masters program, my preceptor gave me my first indication that the corporate world was different than the classroom. During our weekly meeting he told me that he felt I was very bright and I was able to pick up new concepts quickly and apply them. He commented on how I completed all of my assignments in a timely manner without error. However, he wanted to offer me a valuable piece of advice: Don't complete them in such a timely manner. You can imagine my confusion from my preceptor, CEO of the hospital telling me a health administration student that I should intentionally delay completing work that I could complete sooner. Once he explained why it actually made sense. He told me that no one knows the intricacies of what you are working on but you 99% of time because that's how delegation works. The person that gave you the assignment doesn't know all of the efforts that will be needed to complete the project, only what the deliverables of the project are and when it has to be completed. With this in mind, Jeff told me that completing your assignments quickly will give off the impression that the work was extremely straightforward, didn't require much use of resources, skills, and competencies and was basically low hanging fruit. Therefore, you won't receive as much credit for completing the assignment because the PERCEPTION will be that it was easy, and if it was easy, anyone else could have turned it around equally as fast. Now if you take longer on the assignment, engage in some status update e-mails with the manager and discuss what you are doing, what has been completed, and difficulties that you've encountered throughout the life of the project, this gives the impression that the project required you to use your current skills and competencies and perhaps some new ones you've acquired. Also it will give the impression that it was a difficult assignment to complete and that it required a great effort from you to complete before the given deadline. This effort will be looked at favorably as it took you a couple of weeks to complete, you ran into several difficulties, and yet you still completed the project. Now the funny thing is this: The second approach could have taken the same amount of real time as the first approach to complete however no one knows that but you and if the leaders believe that you worked harder it will ultimately help you in your efforts to progress up the ladder. Now I will give you some of my top tips on how to make Perception being Reality work for you and benefit from it:

Tip #1: Arrive 15 minutes early, leave 15 minutes late: This is a great yet simple way to give the perception to your boss and your co-workers that you are dedicated to your work and enjoy it to the point where you don't countdown to 5pm to sprint out of the door because you can't take it anymore.

Tip #2: Always keep work on your desk and on your screen: This will give everyone that passes by your cube or comes into your office the impression that you are not utilizing work time for non work activities. Spreadsheets and Word documents are excellent choices as these can be consistently reviewed, edited, and updated. Also keep reading materials, a legal pad, pen, and highlighter on your desk at all times

Tip #3: Lean forward, not backward in your chair: Leaning forward looks as if you are actively working on something at desk. Leaning backwards could give off the impression that you are chilling. Again no one is going to know that you are chilling because you just got finished completing a tedious analysis, typed 5 policies and procedures, or finished a 2 hour conference call; all they will see is you leaning back looking as if you are watching football on a Sunday. Lean forward!

2. Rules of Engagement

The Webster's definition of Engaged is to be greatly interested or committed and to be involved in activity (Webster, 2014). This word may not mean a lot to you when you are by yourself in your office or at your cube working on your day to day activities because your level of engagement will be evidenced by the projects and/or assignments you complete and how well you accomplish your goals. Engagement in group settings however is extremely important. Only you truly know how interested you are in being in a finance meeting that doesn't impact you at all or the kick off meeting for a process improvement project that you suggested to upper management. However, the way you behave in these settings allows your co-workers, managers, and directors to form an opinion on your level of engagement based on what they perceive the actions of an engaged person to be. Remember PERCEPTION is REALITY in the Corporate Jungle. The person that is taking notes copiously could be no more interested in the subject matter being discussed as a person that is leaning back in their chair with head in hand. However, those around you perceive one set of actions to represent engagement and the other set to represent a lack of engagement. So with this in mind here are a few ways to appear engaged in a group setting:

Tip #1: Be Engaged: Simple enough right. The best thing you can do to actually appear engaged in a group setting is to actively listen to what is being said and pay attention. As much as you may think the weekly meetings for an hour are pointless and nothing gets accomplished, it's your job to be there and they actually pay you for it so don't think about how you need a big game from Adrian Peterson to win your fantasy football game, the season finale of the Bachelor, or what you are going to have for dinner, focus as best you can on what is being said.

Tip #2: Lean forward onto the table: Similar to the imagery leaning forward at your desk provides to anyone that passes your office or desk, leaning forward gives the impression that are very interested in what whoever has the floor is saying. Leaning back in the chair could potentially give the impression the subject matter is boring you and that you have mentally checked out.

Tip #3: Make eye contact with the speaker and take notes: This could have been tip 2.5 because it goes hand and hand with leaning forward. Making eye contact with the speaker shows that you are paying attention and taking notes shows that you are listening and comprehending what is being said.

Tip #4: ASK QUESTIONS: I saved this one for last and put it in all caps because this is the single, greatest way to show that you are engaged in the discussion is to ask questions. Now do not, I repeat DO NOT just ask a question or questions for the sake of asking them. However if it is something you truly don't know or would like to know more about ask! If you are new asking for clarification on acronyms are the perfect low hanging fruit. Every organization has their own nomenclature so asking what it all means is the perfect way to show you are actively listening and want to take something away from the meeting. Don't worry about asking a stupid question because the drawback of not asking a question is greater than the drawback of asking what you feel is a stupid question.

3. Visibility

Brock Lesnar, former UFC Heavyweight Champion, lost his first UFC fight by 1st round submission leading many to call the former pro wrestling champion's foray into MMA as joke because he didn't possess the skills needed to be successful. In his 2nd fight, Lesnar dominated en route to a unanimous decision victory and in the post-fight interview the first words out of Brock's mouth was a question: " Can you see me now?!" This was Brock's way of addressing his detractors who doubted his skills as a MMA fighter that had no choice but to acknowledge them now after such a dominant display over a seasoned MMA fighter. The question "Can you see me now?"

should be the question you pose to your boss through your performance on the projects you are assigned. The best way to increase your visibility is to work on projects that matter to management and upper management. Now this doesn't mean that you reject projects that don't fit this criteria because the most important thing to do when you're new is to get experience, build trust, and establish a reputation. However if you are in a meeting and you hear about a team being put together to complete a project that the CEO has designated as high priority with substantial financial impact that you feel you could play a contributing role in get attached to it. These types of project are excellent ways for you to enhance your learning while increasing your visibility to upper management. Here are some ways to spot projects that could increase your visibility:

Large Financial Investment: Any project that is mentioned that will require a large financial investment from the organization is all but guaranteed to be a project that upper management will have their eyes on. This is because they will be highly interested in Return on

Investment from the project. Large financial investments could be opening of a new service, a large capital purchase, acquisition or merger. Assisting on these projects in a contributing role can get you great exposure.

New technology implementation: These are usually important and call for multidisciplinary teams to complete. This will give you exposure to not only senior leadership but other leaders throughout the company in different areas. Having an endorsement from several managers and directors can have as much impact as a single senior leader endorsement.

Annual fundraisers: These may not appear to be important projects but these are great opportunities for exposure. Playing a pivotal role of bringing in a large gift from a donor or managing the annual fundraiser for the organization will give you exposure to all parts of the organization as well as to external community partners and possibly even the board of directors.

Major Site visit preparation: A lot of industries have routine site visits that are either to keep accreditation/certification or regulatory/compliance visits. These visits are extremely important because no organization wants to be known throughout their industry as having bombed one of these visits. Playing a part in the preparation to be up to par for a site visit is a big deal and can help you gain some visibility.

4. Goals and Expectations

Goals and expectations are the bread and butter of how you will be evaluated in your job. These are the things that you will be expected to deliver at the end of a specific period of time (Monthly, Quarterly, Annually, etc.). Some of your goals and expectations will have been presented to you in your job description you read before applying for the job and during the interview process. However, often times this list does not fully represent all that is expected of you. A good manager/leader will tell you exactly what is expected of you and by when. A bad manager will be less forthcoming with such information and/or will not to the best job of explaining the goals and expectations in enough detail. Since knowing and understanding your goals and expectations is extremely important to your success in your current position but also to your planned upward mobility, I will give you some tips to address Goals and Expectations and to make sure you fully understand what is expected of you.

Tip #1: Ask your boss!: If you have any questions on your deliverables, do not just work aimlessly under the belief that you will accomplish your goals and perform as expected. If your boss does not explicitly detail what your goals and expectations are and when you need to have certain projects completed, ask them and don't accept vague answers. If after the initial explanation you are still unclear, ask again until you are clear and have a full understanding of where your efforts should be directed. There is nothing worse than investing a lot of resources into something that won't help you accomplish a goal or meet expectations.

Tip #2: Write them down: Once you have established what your goals and expectations are, write them down and keep track of them. There are several ways you can do this: making an Excel spreadsheet, creating a personal dashboard, writing them on a dry erase board, or typing them into a Word document and posting them in your cube or office. Never lose sight of your goals and monitor your progress on completing each one. This will help you to manage your time the best way possible to complete all of your goals by the specified due date for each goal.

Tip #3: Share progress with boss: This is a great way to showcase your accomplishments while also reporting roadblocks that have prevented you from achieving your goals. Routinely reach out to your boss and provide status updates. This will make your semi-annual or annual review a much less stressful ordeal for you because you and your boss will know how you performed and what prevented you from performing better.

5. Protect Yourself At All Times

The cardinal rule in the sport of boxing is to protect yourself at all times. The means no matter what may be happening in the ring or at what time during the round, never let your guard down! This is the same attitude that you should have with all of your dealings in Corporate America. Regardless of how cool you think that one co-worker is or how nice your boss seems to be not all of these sentiments are genuine and heartfelt. Some of these people have ulterior motives and are looking to set you up to throw you under the bus, take credit for your work, or make you their own personal helper. This statement is not meant to make you paranoid and feel that everyone who's nice to you at your job is ultimately out to get you because this is simply not the case. However, you should take certain strides to protect yourself just in case and I will provide you some ways to do so.

Tip #1: Document everything: Everyone has a preferred method of contact: some like the phone, others like face-to-face, and others e-mail. Your preferred method of contact should be email because it provides a paper trail of not only what was said but who said it. This can be critical in the future if a person seeks to blame shift or not give you proper credit. If you have a hallway meeting or phone conversation, document what was discussed in your work journal and send a confirmation e-mail confirming the details of the conversation for your clarity. Maintain records and don't be afraid to reference them if needed.

Tip #2: Follow up phone or in-person conversations with a confirmation e-mail: Nothing is worse than being in a he said, she said situation at the workplace. Therefore if your boss asks you to do something or tells you do something in a classic hallway conversation or during a phone call, always confirm what was discussed in an e-mail. That way you will have evidence of the marching orders if that person happens to forget or flat out chooses to not acknowledge that the conversation of interest ever occurred.

Tip #3: Check with your boss before you commit to anything: Depending on your environment and culture this is extremely important. Most professional organizations have transitioned away from the traditional silo format where every department worked independently of each other and kept to themselves to a more synergistic approach where each department views themselves as team members and cogs in the greater machine that is the organization. With this new mindset comes invitations to participate on various multidisciplinary project teams or task force. While this is an excellent way to gain exposure throughout the organization, never accept an invitation to participate on these teams or take on assignments from other managers without getting prior approval from your boss. This will ensure that you are given proper credit for the work you do and will also prevent you from working on something your boss didn't want you working on. Ask for permission instead of forgiveness.

6. Communication

Communication is widely regarded as one of the cornerstones of a successful relationship romantic or otherwise. And in the corporate environment communication is equally as important to your success as professional. There are several ways you can communicate within the corporate environment from the old school traditional options (Phone and In-Person) or newer options (E-mail and Instant Messaging). With all of these tools available everyone has a preferred method of communication. Some like e-mail for record keeping and referral purposes, others like phone calls and instant messaging for the ability to get instant feedback, and others prefer to meet face to face. You as a professional will more than likely have to identify your preferred method of communication but the most important thing for you to identify is the preferred communication of those you work with especially your boss. The reason this is important is because you want to make sure you are communicating as effective and efficiently as possible to prevent delays that will ultimately impact your work. You don't want to waste time trying to schedule a meeting with your boss when they would rather you just call them or e-mail them. You also don't want to repeatedly send your boss emails that don't get responded to when they prefer to meet face to face or over the phone. This should be one of the first things you should find out from your boss and here are some ways to do it:

Tip #1: Ask! The shortest distance between two points is a straight line and with this thinking in mind, if you want to know a person's preferred method just ask them.

Tip #2: Observation: If you ask someone about their preferred method of communication and they say something to the effect of "I don't have a preferred method of communication" it will become a little more challenging to identify the best way to communicate with them. In a situation like this, observe how they communicate with you and their response rate to you with the various forms of communication. For example if you send an email that doesn't get a response in a week but your voicemails are returned promptly, you should stick with using phone calls as the way to get in contact with that person. Sometime trial and error is the only way to go.

7. Surviving the Game

Gatorade once famously had an ad that said "Life is a Sport, drink it up." If you sit down and really think about it, life certainly is a sport. Think about it: you have to improve your skills to be successful, there are several games that must be played through each season, and preparation is paramount to your success. This chapter is one of the most important of the book because this is where we discuss the ins and outs of Corporate America which is the Game. In order to be successful at the game you must first come to the realization that you are in fact playing a game, just like everyone else in Corporate America is. Failure to acknowledge or play the game will ensure you will not achieve your goals or desired level of success. Now I am not telling you this to make you paranoid or give you a heighten sense of anxiety about working in Corporate America. I am educating you on this for that you will be prepared to deal with some things that may come your way by either anticipating them happening or preparing contingency plans in the event they occur. Corporate America is a game of chess not checkers. As in any game there are several factors that you must be knowledgeable about and prepared for to be successful. For example in football a coach would have to be knowledgeable about the rules of the game, the opposing team's scheme, personnel, strengths, and weaknesses as well as his own team's strengths and weaknesses. For example, if a team routinely places 8 men in the box to stop the run, it may be a good idea to take advantage of having less defenders in coverage by passing. The factors that you need to take into account and must constantly monitor to ensure you are successful are: Rules, Players, Tendencies, Competencies, and Opportunities.

Rules: The first things to learn before you engage in any competition are the rules. The rules for the Corporate Game are the culture of the organization and management style of your boss. These are two things that you want a firm grasp on before you accept an offer of employment. If you value having a good work-life balance, working for a company that features 50+ hour work weeks for you will put you in a position to not be successful.

Players: In the Corporate game the players are your managers, peers, directors, and executives. Each of these individuals will have certain characteristics, skills, attributes, and tendencies. How well you pay attention to and learn about the players can determine how successful you will be. It is important to understand each player in order to figure out how to best play with them to achieve your goals.

Tendencies: Each of the players in the game has tendencies that you need to pay attention to and learn in order to be successful. This will go a long way toward ensuring your efforts are not wasted and have the desired impact. For example, a person that is direct and detail-oriented wouldn't want to receive work that's devoid of detailed and unfocused. A person that is not forthcoming with critical details about a project may have to be asked several follow up questions when a project is assigned to you to ensure you fully understand what your expectations are. Knowing the tendencies of the players is paramount to your success in the game.

Competencies: Each player has a particular set of competencies or skills that help them to excel in their position. It is important for you to learn the skills and competencies of those around you as this can come in handy when working on projects and assignments. For example, if you are given a project that involves financial calculations and you are not proficient in this area it will help to save time by working with a team member that has strong financial skills. Additional benefits will be assurance that the correct information is presented and the opportunity to learn how to complete such calculations in the future if necessary.

Opportunities: In every game of every sport there will be openings where a team or player can take advantage of them to ultimately win the game. Most sports use the analogy of a window to describe the best chances for a team to reach their ultimate goal of winning a championship. In Corporate America, there are also windows that will appear that if you are able to climb through them will benefit your professional development and career growth. Opportunities could take many forms such as working on a high visibility project that will get you exposure to key members of the management team. If you are interested in working in a new department or on a new team, a good opportunity would be any projects or assignments that involve the leadership of your desired new team or department to showcase your abilities. This will also give you a level of recognition with leadership if you apply to that position. These examples are just a few of the opportunities that you should be keep your eyes, ears, and minds open for that could help reach the next rung of the corporate ladder.

Tip: Create a career progression plan which includes details of short term and long term professional goals and the steps you will take to accomplish each. This will give you some direction on the opportunities that you should take advantage of so when/if they present themselves, you can show some initiative and pounce on them.

8. The Dangers of Yes

Once you start a new job and have completed your training the projects and assignments usually start to roll in. The project mostly will come from your managers as they will want to assign you projects that will supplement your training and give you some practical experience with what you have learned. Depending on how well you are acclimating yourself to the work you will have the opportunity to work on more projects and assignments. In a later chapter I will discuss the importance of taking initiative and seeking out new projects and assignments. Initiative is a good thing however taking initiative DOES NOT mean saying yes to everything you are offered or asked to do and NEVER agree to take on a project or assignment without knowing the requirements. The dangers of saying yes to everything include overwhelming yourself due to an unbearable workload, working on meaningless assignments, or becoming someone's personal assistant.

If you can take on more work and complete it thoroughly then by all means accept more assignments. However if you feel that you are unable to give the new project the attention it will need for you do produce quality results because of your other work, turn it down. Taking on a lot of projects and completing them won't work in your favor if the quality of your work suffers due to the volume of work you have. It's best to take fewer projects and provide A-level work and results than to take on a lot of projects and provide C- level work and results. Like the old saying goes " Don't bite off more than you can chew."

I discussed in a previous chapter about taking on projects and assignments that will get you exposure and visibility. While not all of your projects will provide high visibility you should monitor the amount of the meaningless projects and assignments you agree to complete. A couple of menial projects are fine but be careful of accepting a lot of these types of project. A meaningless project is a project that provides no visibility, learning opportunity or use of your skill and competencies. You have probably heard these types of projects and assignments referred to as "Busy Work". If you find that a lot of the projects and assignments you are being offered could be completed by someone that has no formal training or skills, decline them until something better comes along. If you're going to work on something, it should be something that either gets you noticed, makes your better, or both.

The most dangerous pitfall of always saying yes is unknowingly becoming someone's personal assistant. This danger is usually limited to taking work from another manager or team member. I mentioned this before but I'll reiterate here, never take any work from someone besides your boss without clearing it with your boss first. Also be careful of people on your team trying to unload undesirable assignments on to you by dressing them up to be more than what they are. Again always ask for details on the projects being offered and if you don't want to take it on or cannot take it on, decline it. Don't be the dumping grounds for another person!

9. Culture is Key

The Webster's definition of Culture is a way of thinking, behaving, or working that exists in a place or organization (Websters, 2014). The culture of an organization is basically how the organization conducts their business. Each organization has their own culture that you will be expected to conform to upon accepting a position with that organization. Not all organizational cultures will be conducive to your style of work or your preferences. For example, if you are a creative person that values being innovative, it wouldn't be the best fit for you to work in a culture that doesn't value innovation and doesn't allow you to use your creativity. An organization's and team's culture should be one the most important factors you should consider in choosing an organization. There are many aspects of an organization's culture that you should consider before applying for positions within that organization but I will address a few of the more important ones.

- Work-life balance: The importance that an organization places on the work-life balance of their employees is extremely important. Some modern organizations created ways to improve the work-life balance of employees by using flexible schedules, the ability to work from home, and capping the amount of Personal Time Off (PTO) hours you can carry over from year to year. By capping the amount of hours you can carry over, an organization forces employees to take time off or lose their hours for nothing. The best way to find out how an organization feels about work-life balance is to ask your manager about the hours and days you're expected to work per week and to discuss PTO with a human resources representative. It might not be the best idea to talk about time off with your manager because you don't want to have them question your dedication to the job and give them reason to worry about your attendance. If your manager tells you that the team members routinely work more than 50 hours per week and you feel this is too much, you should consider other positions at another organization.

- Strict vs.Relaxed: A strict culture is one in which there is little to no flexibility or give as it pertains to protocol and procedure. In a strict culture is not just about how you are performing in your job, it's also about how you are fitting into the culture and being a living reflection of it. A relaxed culture is one in which there is more flexibility and completed projects, assignments, and goals are the most important thing although there are protocol and procedure you must follow. The example of a strict culture is one in which you probably are penalized for being late to work over a certain amount time regardless of circumstances, your lunch times are tracked heavily, and there may not be a lot of flexibility in work hours and dress code. For example, if you have 30 minutes to eat lunch and you take a 35 minute lunch, chances are you are going to hear about this and if it happens enough it could result in disciplinary action. A relaxed culture will be one where that 35 minute lunch will not result in a disciplinary action however this doesn't mean you can take an hour lunch each day and that will be ok. In this positions if you have to be late on a certain day, you can make the time up without using PTO hours. Also as long as you work at least 40 hours in a work week, you're cool. So if you happen to stay late a couple of days and you want to leave out a little early (keywords: a little), that's fine. My advice to you is to play everything close to the vest until you feel you have a great handle on whether your culture is strict or relaxed. Get to work a little early, stay a little late and come back from lunch on time or early. That way if a culture is strict you won't be getting in any trouble.

- Growth Opportunities: A term you may often thrown around in Corporate America is upward mobility. Upward mobility means the ability you have to move up the ranks within the organization. A lot of organizations today prefer to build from within by promoting internal staff to manager and director positions instead of bringing in leaders from the outside. The average modern day professional changes jobs every 3-5 years so if you are in an organization that does not have many opportunities for growth, chances are you will have to leave the organization to further your career and take those next steps up the corporate ladder. This would mean basically starting over within a new organization and giving up all of the perks you may have acquired by working within an organization for 3-5 year. If you would rather grow upwards within an organization one of the aspects of the culture you will want to check for is opportunity for growth.

- Professional Development: Professional development is the level of support an organization has for employees seeking to better themselves as professionals. This could include tuition reimbursement for gaining additional education or certification, paying for annual fees to professional organizations, and covering the cost for professional conferences that may benefit you in your position. An organization that doesn't place a high value on professional development will be less willing to provide financial support for the things listed above so make sure to do your research on the organization's benefits.

10. Impact of Initiative

Synonyms of initiative include action, aggressiveness, ambition, drive, go, and hustle, all of which you will need to exhibit in order to be successful in Corporate America. Initiative is one of the most attributes that your managers will be looking for in you. Do you have the ambition to challenge yourself or do you need you be challenged by your boss? Is your drive high enough that you will see a problem and proactively start to think about solutions to it or will you sit back and wait until you are told it's a problem? As I mentioned earlier taking initiative does not mean always saying yes or taking on every project offered to you. Instead effectively taking initiative is taking on the projects and assignments that will help increase your visibility within the organization, enhance your learning, and will assist in accomplishing departmental, team, and/or organizational goals.

Tip#1: Proactively ask for work: This is one of the best and most productive ways to take initiative. You are paid to work and be there for at least 8 hours so it's best to keep yourself busy while you are there to make those 8 hours go by that much faster. If you notice your project lists starting to dwindle, drop your boss a quick e-mail saying that you are at point now where you are able to take on more assignments. This will help keep you busy, further enhance your learning, and exhibit your engagement and drive within the position. In addition to asking your boss for work, reach out to other team members to see if they need assistance with anything. This is a great way to further your learning while exhibiting that you are a team player.

Tip#2: Provide solutions to team/departmental problems: No team or department is perfect which means there are ways to improve overall team performance. Another great way to exhibit initiative is to think about solutions to problems that affect the efficiency and effectiveness of the department. This could be tweaking a process that the team members use to complete their work or suggesting a training opportunity that could help to improve performance. A great way to get started on this is to ask yourself the following questions: What are some things that would make me more efficient and effective in my position?

How could this be done easier? Chances are someone else in the department have thought about this but didn't put the effort in to develop a solution. If you manage to create a solution that will make life easier on the department, it will be a great feather in your cap.

11. Mentors

The reason I wrote this book was to provide guidance to those that are preparing to take the plunge into Corporate America. However I am unable to be available to you on a consistent basis to ask questions and bounce ideas off of and this is why you need a mentor. A mentor is a very important asset to have in your quest to be successful in Corporate America. Your mentor will be the person that will serve as a sounding board when you have issues and a knowledge source when you need advice. Your mentor should be a professional that has enjoyed some success in Corporate America and has more experience than you. Here are some good ways to find mentor candidates:

Tip#1: Alumni network: All colleges and universities have alumni networks and associations that allow alumni to stay informed about what is happening at their alma mater currently as well as the successes of their classmates and other alumni. Some schools have alumni directories where you can search for alumni by year of graduation, location, or occupation and includes some contact information. This is an excellent way to find alumni that are in the field that you want to get into or are currently in. Search the directory and start sending out emails. Once you have made the initial contact and receive a response, take the responsibility to keep the dialogue going. Also don't stop at just one, if multiple people are willing to mentor you accept it, you never know what could come from it. Like the saying goes, sometimes it's not what you know, it's who you know.

Tip#2: Networking Events: In addition to your alumni network, professional networking events are also a great way to meet potential mentors. Research professional organizations that maybe specific to your industry such as the American Society of Quality or local professional organizations in your city. Get out and network with people in your field and see what happens.

Tip#3: Former Bosses: Another great source for mentors is a former boss. A former boss is great mentor because they are well aware of your strengths and areas of improvement so the advice they give you will be crafted personally for you instead of being generic. Also they will be able to guide you in the right direction based on the goals they know you want to achieve.

Conclusion

If you have made it to this point I would like to thank you for taking time out to read this book. I didn't write this to end up on the New York Times Bestsellers Lists or to start my career as an author. I wrote this book because through the trials and tribulations I have personally experienced during my time in Corporate America I wished someone would have told me about some Corporate America basics such as the ones I have shared with you. If one person reads this book and has an easier time making the transition from classroom to conference then my mission has been accomplished. I hope this book becomes a great resource that you can use throughout your career and share with your peers and future mentees. In conclusion, I would like to leave you with a quote that in my opinion perfectly encompasses the spirit of Corporate America and it comes from Omar Little from the critically acclaimed show The Wire: " The game is out there. Either you play or get played." Happy hunting people!

Thank You

First and foremost, I want to thank God for all of the successes and failures that allowed me to complete this book. I would like to thank my mom and dad for always supporting me in anything I ever chose to do. Thank you to my brothers Gabe and Darnell for all of their support and advice throughout my career and for pushing me to step outside of myself. Thank you to my lady Akilah for her support and encouragement to write this book and share it with the world. Much love to you all!

Lastly thank you to everyone that has helped me in any way, shape, form, or fashion in my professional career, it was and is greatly appreciated.

Sources Cited

Merriam-Webster Dictionary (2014). http://www.merriam-webster.com/

www.ingramcontent.com/pod-product-compliance
Lightning Source LLC
LaVergne TN
LVHW021626080426
835510LV00019B/2781